FOR WORLD PEACE AND UNIFICATION • USA

Guide to the
Seonghwa Ceremony

Prepared by the District One
Seonghwa Committee

2016

Table of Contents

Gone From My Sight

I am standing upon the seashore. A ship, at my side, spreads her white sails to the moving breeze and starts for the blue ocean. She is an object of beauty and strength.

I stand and watch her until, at length, she hangs like a speck of white cloud just where the sea and sky come to mingle with each other.

Then, someone at my side says, "There, she is gone." Gone where?

Gone from my sight. That is all. She is just as large in mast, hull and spar as she was when she left my side. And, she is just as able to bear her load of living freight to her destined port.

Her diminished size is in me -- not in her.

And, just at the moment when someone says, "There, she is gone," there are other eyes watching her coming, and other voices ready to take up the glad shout, "Here she comes!"

And that is dying...

Henry Van Dyke (1852 – 1933)

Summary of the Seonghwa Ceremony

Prepared by District One Seonghwa Ministry Committee

This summary is offered as an aid to our Blessed families. Ascension to the Spirit World is part of the three stages of life that our True Parents have taught us. Therefore, members should consider simple steps to prepare for our inevitable graduation to life in the Spirit World. Preparation suggestions: (1) Talk to your family about this subject. (2) Prepare a will. (3) Fill out an advance directive and living will. (4) Purchase a plot at the National Wonjeon Shrine of America at Fort Lincoln Cemetery in Bladensburg, MD.

THE MEANING OF SEONGHWA*: The Seonghwa ceremony is the celebration of the commencement of one's life as an exclusively spiritual being. According to the Principle, the Seonghwa ceremony is to be regarded as more beautiful, enlightening, and joyful than even the Blessing ceremony. The Seonghwa tradition was taught by our True Parents after the ascension of their son, Heung Jin Moon, in 1984.*

THREE PHASES OF THE SEONGHWA CEREMONY*: The Seonghwa ceremony has three phases: Ghihwan, Seonghwa, and Wonjeon:*

Ghihwan ("returning to joy")*. The farewell greetings that the immediate family share with the ascended spirit. The purpose is to invite the ascended member to strive for joy, happiness and thankfulness. This ceremony may take place in the hospital, hospice, home, or funeral home.*

Seonghwa ("heavenly harmony")*. The service held with family, friends, and community. The ceremony takes place three, five, or seven days after the person ascends. It is the final farewell ceremony for the departing spirit and may be considered as a "passport" to the Spiril World.*

Wonjeon ("returning home to the palace")*. The ceremony at the burial site. The Wonjeon ceremony sends the body back to its place of origin and is part of the interment ceremony. Wonjeon* *can be defined as the physical body returning to its home, that is, the earth.*

These three phases of the Seonghwa take place over the course of three, five, or seven days (an odd number of days). Day one is the day of death. Memorial services may be offered at the Wonjeon — 3, 21, 40, and 100 days after the ascension. When offering a prayer at the memorial service, pray that the ascended person can lead a good life in the eternal Spirit World centered on God's will.

~ Prepared by the District One Seonghwa Committee

**True Father's Universal Seonghwa,
September 15, 2012**

Introduction

This guide is offered as an aid to families in planning the Seonghwa ceremony. The time of ascension is emotionally challenging for families and friends, and it is hoped that this manual will lessen the stress and give families reassurance that they are doing everything possible to support the person who is ascending.

We hope that this guide will also encourage Blessed members to discuss with family and friends their wishes concerning their Seonghwa in advance, "for we know not the day nor the hour." If we truly understand the substantial reality of the spiritual world and the meaning of the Seonghwa, then we should plan for it joyfully and openly.

The following information is a combination of the ceremony described in *The Tradition, Book One*, and oral tradition since that book was published more than 30 years ago. It provides checklists and advice on planning the service and supporting the family.

This guide does not claim to be the final word on the Seonghwa tradition. In talking to various people who have extensive experience with Seonghwas, we found that there were variations in what was believed to be "essential" vs. "recommended" aspects and Unification vs. Oriental tradition, as well as the practical and feasible.

Please know that the most important element of a Seonghwa is attitude: love, honor, and respect for the individual and joyfully releasing the individual to begin his or her life as an exclusively spiritual being.

The Principle way of dealing with death, or as Unificationists say, ascension, is one part of a larger philosophy of life in which true reality is recognized as having two dimensions: physical <u>and</u> spiritual. God created men and women as the microcosm of the Physical World and the Spirit World. In Unification tradition, the greatest consideration and respect is accorded the ascended.

Funerary customs are supervised in Unificationist communities by a Seonghwa Committee, composed of volunteers to aid the bereaved and to ensure that appropriate practices are followed. When a member of a community dies, it is the community's responsibility to lovingly assist the deceased's family in this act of respect. The Seonghwa Committee is prepared to assist families in making arrangements with a funeral home and to advise them concerning traditional practices and requirements.

The family needs support during this time and people to help organize the ceremony. An ad hoc committee may be formed that can include the pastor, community leader, and friends. It is suggested that someone be designated as the coordinator to organize and delegate people for the prayer vigil and handle donations, food, accommodations and logistics for out-of-town family and guests, as well as the Seonghwa ceremony.

True Parents spoke frequently about death and the need to prepare for its eventuality. In particular, Father directed that members should write an autobiography as a first-person account of living in the Age of the Lord of the Second Advent.

It is suggested that members organize their photographs (digitize and label them) and historic memorabilia. These represent a heartfelt legacy and memorial to be left to our loved ones and descendants.

Also, True Parents have called on all Blessed families to make their ancestors in the Spirit World into absolute good spirits by completing the liberation and Blessing ceremonies through the Cheongpyeong Heaven and Earth Training Center.

Always remember, our time in the Physical World is preparation for life in the Spirit World, the eternal world of God. So before that transition occurs, it is important to resolve our differences and disagreements. We should be able to say to all our loved ones: Please forgive me. I forgive you. Thank you, and I love you.

~ Prepared by the District One Seonghwa Committee

Rev. Ernest Patton, Rev. Zagery Oliver, Rev. Andrew Love, Rev. Gregg Jones, Rev. Randall Francis, Rev. Greg Carter, and Dr. William Selig

Organ Donation and Cremation

In 2013, on the first anniversary of True Father's Seonghwa ceremony, Dr. Chang Shik Yang met with True Mother and specifically asked about organ donation and cremation. True Mother said: "It is good but with conditions." Dr. Yang said she definitely approves of organ donation and considers it a sacrificial act and an example of living for the sake of others. Mother said, "If possible, the recipient should know that the organ is from a Blessed One and that by receiving the organ they are receiving the Blessing from True Parents with the responsibility to build God's kingdom." So, if feasible, the recipient or the donor should be made aware before the organ transfer, but if it's an emergency decision, then Mother says it's always a blessing to help another person. On his own driver's license, Dr. Yang said he marked himself as an organ donor.

Regarding cremation, according to the *Tradition* (published in 1985), "The practice of cremation is not in accordance with the Unification view, as it does not allow the physical body a natural return to the physical (material) world." However, True Mother told Dr. Yang, "Cremation is very common in Korea nowadays. With a prayerful attitude, place the ashes in an urn or in the ground or spread them at the base of a tree so they can nourish the earth."

Whether to choose a traditional burial or cremation is the family's choice. Cremation is popular in Korea and Japan. What's important at the farewell / returning home ceremony — whether it is done with cremated remains or with an intact body — is the heart and motivation. If the ceremony is done with a spirit of understanding, compassion, dignity, and love, then it will be received by our Heavenly Parent.

The Cheongpyeong Heaven and Earth Training Center conveyed the following instruction from Daemonim regarding cremation. If the choice is cremation, then members should offer a sincere "heartfelt prayer to Heaven," and report the Blessed member's full name, birthdate, age, and reason of passing to Cheongpyeong immediately after the ascension and, if possible, before the cremation. For non-Blessed individuals, steps should be taken by family and friends to guide the ascended one to complete both the Ancestor Liberation and Blessing Ceremony.

Daemonim has pledged to protect and comfort the spirit being throughout the ascension, and send Absolute Good Ancestors to bring the individual to Heung Jin Nim's Special Training Center and then to the Unification Spirit Sphere[1] (Unification Realm of the Spirit World). Our attitude, according to Daemonim, should be to console the family and support its decision. The Principle attitude and way is to comfort the heart with compassion and selfless love. For further information: http://eng.cheongpyeong.org/index.asp or email the International office at treeofblessing@gmail.com.

Family members place flowers on True Father's casket.

---

[1] The expression "Unification Spirit Sphere" was used in True Father's Universal Seonghwa program, September 15, 2012. Dr. Sang Hun Lee (1914-1997) had previously used the term, "Unification Realm of the Spirit World."

The Meaning of Seonghwa

The Seonghwa ceremony is the celebration of the commencement of one's life as an exclusively spiritual being. According to True Father, the ceremony is to be regarded as more beautiful, enlightening, and joyful than even the Blessing ceremony.[2]

Father shared some thoughts about its significance on the occasion of Heung Jin Nim's ascension ceremony at Belvedere on January 7, 1984. His comments were printed in the January-February 1984 issue of *Today's World.*

> I'd like to make a very clear announcement that will set the tradition of our movement and our church. In the secular world, death signifies the end of life. However, in our world, death is like a rebirth or a new birth into another world, particularly for those who give their life for the purpose of the Kingdom of Heaven and for the sake of the movement.
>
> For that reason, we must not make those occasions gloomy or sad or feel discouraged. Instead, we shall rejoice in the victory of the spirit in which that life was given for the mission. If we here on earth become very mournful and gloomy, it is like pulling the person who is going up to the heavens down to the ground.
>
> This is a birth from the second universal mother's womb into another world, just like when a baby emerges from its first mother's womb.
>
> A Seung Hwa ceremony is actually comparable to a wedding, when men and women get married. It's not a sorrowful occasion at all. It's like an insect coming out of its cocoon, getting rid of a shackle,

---

[2] In 2011, on the occasion of the passing of early disciple David Sang Chul Kim, Father modified the "Seunghwa" ceremony and referred to it as the "Seonghwa" ceremony. The meaning was clarified to mean not only "ascension and harmony," but to mean "heavenly harmony," a sublime change, perhaps like the evaporation of water—it is still water, but in a different form.

and becoming a new body and a new existence, a new entity. That's exactly the same kind of process.

In our way of life and tradition, Spirit World and Physical World are one, and by our living up to that kind of ideal, we bring the two worlds together into one.

Father's calligraphy for Hong Soon Ae, "Loyalty of Mind, Dedication of Body," November 6, 1989.

Pre-Seonghwa Ceremony

Prayer vigil

An important tradition that takes place in the interim between ascension and the Seonghwa is a prayer vigil. Traditionally, an around-the-clock prayer vigil begins as soon after the ascension as possible and continues until the Seonghwa begins. Variations may include prayers from midnight until 4 a.m. and memorial services in the home or the home of a friend from 8 p.m. to 10 p.m.

Heart and love bring family and friends together, including prayers for and testimonies about the person who passed. When no one is praying, Holy Songs or favorite music may be playing.

Along with Hoondokhae, people can share uplifting stories and accomplishments of the ascended one.

The prayer vigil continues until the Seonghwa Ceremony. It is also good to have some pictures of the person's life: a photo album or other display.

Prayer vigil check list:

- Contact the family and decide where and when to have it

- Send announcement to community

- Clean and Holy Salt the room[3]

- Set up the altar with a small table with a white cloth on it, or Unification or FFWPU flag

- Place on the table an 8" x 10" picture in a nice frame with a white bow and a ribbon

---

[3] Prayer for the purification of items and places with the Cheon Il Guk Holy Salt. "I sanctify (name of item or place) in the name of our Heavenly Parent, the Parents of Heaven and Earth, and (your name), owner of Cheon Il Guk, Aju."

- On the altar: Cheon Il Guk candle and candle holder, Holy Salt, a small bowl with light- colored sand and sticks of incense, and matches

- Fresh flowers on the floor in front of the table or on the table if there is enough space

- Photo of True Parents is only for prayer vigil, not the Seonghwa service.

- Large white sheet may be laid out on the floor in front of the table during the vigil

- CD player with Holy Songs playing can be placed somewhere in the room

- Coordinate the people for each time slot (1 – 2 hours)

- If many people are willing to pray, one-hour slots are possible to fill; however, if not enough people or there will be a long time before the Seonghwa Ceremony, then two-hour slots are more practical

General format

- Light candle, then offer a greeting with a half bow

- Offer incense (optional)

- Holy Songs

- Representative prayer

- Hoondokhae, personal testimonies, and sharing

- Individual prayer

- Closing song

Sample Announcements to the Community

The Seonghwa of (name) will be held at (location, address) on (date) beginning at (time).

http://www.youcaring.com (free online fundraising), if desired.

This fund is being set up in memory of (name), our dear brother who passed away as the result of a (illness) on (date).

Below is a short biography wrote about himself before passing:

Bio ...

***

date

Dear Brothers and Sisters,

(name) unexpectedly passed to the spirit world early this morning after a heart attack at his home in (location).

Bio ....

Please pray and offer support to the family. Details of the Seonghwa and Wonjeon Ceremonies will be finalized and published in the coming days.

signed

***

date

Dear Family,

Here is a recap on what is happening starting tomorrow:

Date, time - Prayer Vigil at the (name) house

Address

15

date, time - Viewing at (name) Funeral Home

There will be an open casket viewing this (date) from 6:30 pm to 8 pm at the Funeral Home in (location) e. All are welcome to offer prayers and love. We welcome members who'd like to bring flowers, single or a bouquet.

Name
Address
City, state, zip
Phone

Date, time - Seonghwa Ceremony at (location)
This special evening will include song, prayer, biography reading, photo slideshow, testimonies, and more. It's a time to reflect on all the positive ways she has affected each of our lives, and to share those memories with each other.

Reception to follow. Refreshments will be provided.

CLOTHING: Wear whatever you feel is appropriate for this occasion, lighter colors recommended. (Traditional seonghwa attire of wearing white not required.)

You may RSVP on Facebook:
(optional)

Donations
Your donations to support the family are greatly appreciated. You may donate online by clicking here:

P.G. Memorial Fund
Online fundraising, if desired.

Checks can be given at any of these events above. Please make them out to (name).

God bless you and your family.

Three Phases of the Seonghwa Ceremony

The Seonghwa ceremony has three phases: Ghihwan, Seonghwa, and Wonjeon:

(1) Ghihwan ("Returning to Joy"). The farewell greetings that the immediate family shares with the ascended spirit. Invite the member to strive for joy, happiness, and thankfulness. This ceremony may take place in the hospital, hospice, home, or funeral home.

(2) Seonghwa ("Heavenly Harmony"). The service held with family, friends, and community. The ceremony takes place three, five, or seven days after the person ascends. It is the final farewell ceremony for the departing spirit and may be considered as a passport to the Unification Spirit Sphere.

(3) Wonjeon ("Returning Home to the Palace"). The ceremony at the burial site. The Wonjeon ceremony sends the body back to its place of origin and is part of the interment ceremony. Wonjeon can be defined as the physical body returning to its home, that is, the earth.

These three phases of the Seonghwa take place over the course of three, five, or seven days (an odd number of days). Day 1 is the day of passing.

Preparation of the body and casket

The price of caskets can range anywhere from $500 to $10,000. Obviously it is the choice of the family, but it should be understood that no casket can fully protect human remains from decomposition no matter how much is spent. By spending more, the inevitable may be delayed, but it won't be avoided indefinitely. Caskets are steel, hardwood, fiberglass, or particleboard with a cloth covering. It is also possible to purchase an inexpensive casket on the Internet. You are not required to buy from the funeral home.

- The casket should be sanctified with Holy Salt before the body is dressed and placed in it.

- Blessed members are prayerfully bathed and dressed in a Holy Robe, white gloves, white underclothes, and white socks or stockings.

In the era of Cheon Il Guk, we need to appreciate the incalculable value of our members and the historical sacred path we have walked. For example, could a monetary value be placed on the Holy Shroud of Turin, which is believed to be the cloth in which Joseph of Arimathea wrapped the body of Jesus? Of course not. The shroud is priceless. Imagine a museum with a handwritten letter by Jesus, a comb, an item of clothing, his carpentry tools, a hammer or chisel, or a chair that he built or even sat in? Such items would be precious beyond all price.

Similarly, shrines and museums will be built by future generations in respect and appreciation of those who lived in the age of the True Parents. Videos, photographs, memorabilia, letters, and especially the Holy Robe and Blessing Ring, which were worn for providential ceremonies (three-day ceremony, pledge with True Parents, etc.) will be held in the highest esteem.

All newly purchased garments need to be Holy Salted. It is important that the robe's belt be tied correctly.

According to *The Tradition*, the Blessing Ring should be left on and buried; however, some members, including the local Seonghwa committee, have chosen to leave this precious heirloom to our loved ones. The choices would be: a) bequeath the ring to our descendants, b) not be buried with a ring, and c) purchase a second ring so one can be buried and the other be a sacred remembrance. White gloves are worn.

Place the following items in the casket:

- Holy handkerchief which was received at the Holy Wine ceremony.

- *Exposition of the Divine Principle*

- Special items that the person may love, particularly for a child; anything placed in the casket should be Holy Salted.

- Second Generation may not have a Holy Gown. The options would be: (a) purchase a Holy Gown, (b) be buried in a dark suit for men or white (or light-colored) dress for women. All newly purchased garments should be sanctified with Holy Salt.

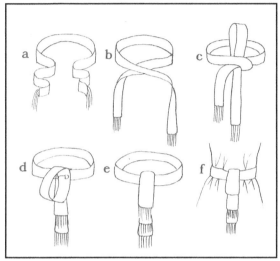

How to tie belt of the Holy Robe

Ghihwan Ceremony
("Returning to Joy")

The Ghihwan ceremony ("Returning to Joy") is a brief memorial service, the farewell greetings that the immediate family, trinity members, spiritual children, spiritual parents, and friends share with the elevated spirit. This means that at some time during the interim between ascension and the Seonghwa, the family and friends visit wherever the body is and offer their prayers and farewell greetings. Our attitude should be one of sincerity and respect. The efforts and dedication of his or her past life on earth should be remembered.

Location. This may take place at the hospital a funeral home, or church center. Family, relatives, and members of the community may pray, sing, offer testimonies, and say their farewells.

If the individual has specified his or her desires in this matter, those desires should be honored, otherwise, decisions are made by the spouse of the ascending spirit (or parents if the ascending spirit is a Blessed child Holy Salt the room where the Ghihwan ceremony takes place. The casket may be open or closed during the Ghihwan ceremony, according to the family's wishes.

Seonghwa Ceremony
("Heavenly Harmony")

Location

The Seonghwa ceremony may be held at a church center; regional or national headquarters, depending on the realm of the ascending individual's life mission or work; someone's home; or a funeral parlor. Visit the place chosen for the Seonghwa as much in advance of the ceremony as possible. Find out what support services are available from the mortuary or church: sound system, lighting, easels, parking. Assign someone as greeter to welcome the guests as they enter the building, guide them to sign the registration book and leave a donation, and give them a program. Assign an usher to escort them to their seat. Family and relatives should be in the front row.

Ceremony time

The time of the ceremony is arranged to accommodate the schedules of the immediate family, the funeral home, and the cemetery.

Dress code

For members of the immediate family and those who have an official role (officiator, pallbearers, picture carrier): Women should wear white or light-colored clothes and red flower corsages. Men should wear dark blue suits with a white shirt and white tie and boutonnieres of white flowers. Pallbearers wear white gloves while carrying the coffin.

Preparation for the ceremony

Holy Salt the room where the Seonghwa ceremony takes place, if possible, prior to the casket being moved into it. If the Ghihwan was in the same room, it is not necessary to Holy Salt again.

Place altar (in front of the casket), including the following items:

- New white or light-colored cloth to cover altar

- Framed picture of individual, in wood frame (14" x 17" is good)

- Pink or white ribbon for picture

Make sure the room is well lit.

Place flower arrangements around the casket and altar.

Prepare single flowers for the flower offering during the Seonghwa. (The same single flowers may be used for the flower offering at the Wonjeon.)

The banner or sign displayed at the front of the room should say something like: "Seonghwa Ceremony of [name of person] [date]."

The advantage of using a banner is that it is easy to fold and cherish as an historical keepsake. The disadvantage is that it can be hard to hang at the Seonghwa site. It is important to visit the site ahead of time to see how the banner could be hung and then to bring the right materials to do so on the day of the ceremony. The advantage of using a sign is that it is often cheaper and doesn't have to be hung. An easel will be needed or other kind of support to display it. When you visit the Seonghwa site, think of where to display the sign (behind the coffin or next to it) and obtain the appropriate size and type of easel. The disadvantage of a sign is it is often fragile and bulky and therefore hard to store. Some copy centers can make a sign on large, good-quality paper that can be mounted on a stiff background such as foam board. Then, depending on how the sign was mounted, it could be removed, rolled, and easily stored.

The Family Federation or Unification Church flag is placed across the casket.

The guest book can be the same guest book used for the Gwihwan ceremony. The member's family keeps this as a remembrance.

Put bowl of Holy Salt at entrance.

The program usually lists the order of service and those participating and may include copies of the songs as an insert. A biography of the individual is often read during the ceremony and a copy could also be included as an insert, if desired.

Arrange for someone to play music for the hymns and for someone to do a musical offering.

The funeral home will have a podium available for the officiator to use.

The Seonghwa ceremony and the Wonjeon ceremony may be photographed and videotaped and given to the immediate family. If no videotaping is done, then at least a photographer should be arranged. The individuals operating the cameras should be sensitive to the situation.

No picture of True Parents or True Family should be used in any part of the ceremony.

The family may choose someone to serve as the service leader, such as a family friend or elder Blessed member. It is not appropriate for the spouse to do so.

Begin the ceremony with songs. These include the Cheon Il Guk Anthem and Holy Songs, or other songs appreciated by the ascending individual. Before the ceremony begins, play music softly in the background.

.A representative prayer is offered by the officiator or someone chosen by the family. Then a short biography of the ascending member and testimonies are shared.

The ascending individual's church leader is introduced by the officiator and delivers a sermon. Of course, if it is the family's wish, someone other than a church leader can give the address.

There are different levels of the Seonghwa ceremony according to the level of the ascended's mission:

- Universal
- World
- Continental

- National
- Regional
- State
- Church

A Universal Seonghwa Ceremony was held for True Father. A World Seonghwa Ceremony was held for the True Children: Heung Jin Nim, Young Jin Nim, and Hyo Jin Nim. National level ceremonies were held for Jin Joo Byrne (1984-2002); David S. C. Kim, founding president of UTS (1915-2011); and Eric Holt, HSA National Treasurer (1952-2013).

Either one by one or in small groups (depending on the number of people involved), those attending the Seonghwa should:

- Express a gesture of respect. Facing altar/casket, offer one full (or half) bow.

- Place a flower on the chest of the ascending individual, or on top of the casket.

- Offer another full or half bow and return to their seats.

If there are too many people, representatives may be chosen. These representatives should be announced by the officiator, making sure to have them come forward in a manner consistent with heavenly hierarchy. This is the general order:

- Members of the immediate family (they are first so they may receive condolences)

- Pastors and community leaders

- Elder Blessed couples (in order of Blessing group)

- Other friends and members

A closing hymn or musical offering usually follows the flower offering.

A closing prayer is offered to end the Seonghwa.

Announce procession guidelines. The officiator or a mortuary representative can explain the mortuary's guidelines for the procession. Usually this entails the drivers turning on car headlights, and sometimes flashers as well, and following the hearse without breaking the procession (proceeding through intersections and stoplights without stopping).

Items to bring from Seonghwa ceremony to burial site.

- Individual's picture and easel to hold photo frame
- Flowers
  - Funeral home arranges for the flowers to be transported in the hearse or van.
  - Individual flowers offered at the end of the ceremony can be brought and used at Wonjeon
- Incense and receptacle [optional]
- Matches or lighter
- Holy Salt
- Tape to secure the flag draped on the coffin
- A simple sound system, if possible.
- Arrange to have or bring a shovel and some loose soil for soil offering

Marker and Sample Inscription

The member's family selects the type of marker. Information that may be inscribed on it: name of individual, dates of birth and ascension, Blessing group, church logo. If True Father bestowed a title such as "Reverend," that should be included.

First and Last Name
2075 Blessing
Birthdate – Ascension date
Words of endearment

26

Sample Template for Seonghwa Program

<u>Front Cover:</u>

In Celebration of the Life of

(name)

Photo

"Heavenly Harmony, Ascension & Returning Home"
(Seonghwa and Wonjeon Ceremonies)

date

Family Federation for World Peace and Unification

Services and Interment at:
Fort Lincoln Cemetery
3401 Bladensburg Rd.
Brentwood, MD 20722

Seonghwa Ceremony for _____
day, date, year

Officiator: _____

Welcome	_____
Cheon Il Guk Anthem	"Blessing of Glory"
Invocation	_____
Musical Offering	_____
Biography	_____
Slide/Video Tribute	_____
Seonghwa Address	_____
Testimonies	_____
	_____
	_____
Family Greeting	_____
Flower Presentation	
Closing Hymn	"Song of the Garden"
Closing Prayer	
Three Cheers of Eog-mansei[4]	_____
Close of Ceremony:	_____

Wonjeon Ceremony
time

Procession to burial site-	
Officiator: _____	
Hymn	"Song of the Garden"
Invocation	_____
Wonjeon Address	_____
Flower Offering	All Attendees
Soil Offering	All Attendees
Benediction	_____
Three Cheers of Eog-mansei	_____

---

[4] Three or four cheers of Eog-mansei: Eok-mansei for the beloved Heavenly Parent! (hanul Pumo nim) Eok-mansei for the victorious True Parents of Heaven, Earth and Humankind! (Cham Pumo nim) Eok-mansei for the establishment of Cheon Il Guk! (Optional 4th cheer, Eok-mansei for (name).

Pages 2-3 can be biography or lyrics. Holy Songs may be downloaded:

http://www.tparents.org/Library/Unification/Topics/Hsong/hsongs.htm

"Seonghwa (Heavenly Harmony) Ceremony"

The ceremony is actually comparable to a wedding, when men and women get married. It's not a sorrowful occasion at all. It's like an insect coming out of its cocoon, getting rid of a shackle and becoming a new body and a new existence, a new entity. That's exactly the same kind of process.

In our way of life and tradition, spirit world and physical world are one, and by our living up to that kind of ideal, we bring the two worlds together into one.

In the secular world, death signifies the end of the life. However in our world, death is like a rebirth or a new birth into another world. For this reason, we should not make those occasions gloomy or sad or feel discouraged.

If we here on earth become very mournful or gloomy, it is like pulling the person who is going up to the heavens down to the earth.

~ Sun Myung Moon

***

Therefore we are always confident and know that as long as we are at home in the body, we are away from the Lord. We live by faith, not by sight. We are confident. I say, and would prefer to be away from the body and at home with the lord. So we make it our goal to please him, whether we are at home in the body or away from it.

~ II Corinthian 5:6-9

Wonjeon Ceremony
("Returning Home to the Palace")

Personnel needed

- Pallbearers. Six to eight pallbearers are chosen prior to the Seonghwa ceremony. Wear dark suits, white ties, and white gloves. Pallbearers carry the casket from the Seonghwa ceremony to the hearse and from the hearse to the Wonjeon site.

- Portrait carrier. One individual is chosen to carry the portrait of the individual from the Seonghwa ceremony to the Wonjeon site. This individual walks ahead of the casket carrying the picture from the Seonghwa to the hearse and from the hearse to the Wonjeon site. The picture should precede the casket at all times. This means that during the journey to the Wonjeon site, the person may ride in the front seat of the hearse (if allowed) holding the picture or the picture is placed on the front seat of the hearse. Men wear the same attire as pallbearers, and women wear white or light-colored clothes and a red flower corsage.

- Holy Salter. One individual is also chosen to Holy Salt the path of the casket from the Seonghwa ceremony to the hearse and from the hearse to the Wonjeon site and the burial site itself. He or she should precede the hearse and Holy Salt the entire route to the Wonjeon and then around the four corners of the Wonjeon grounds. The Holy Salter wears the same attire as the portrait carrier. This is most often the elder church leader of the area.

Procession to burial ground

After the service, the procession to the burial ground should begin. The Holy Salter goes first, followed by the picture bearer, followed by the pallbearers carrying the casket.

The hearse is followed by the vehicles carrying the immediate family. The funeral home can arrange for limos to carry the family to the Wonjeon site. When you choose a funeral home, discuss in detail what services are provided for what price. They often offer "packages" of services, as well as "à la carte" services. Make sure what you choose includes only the services you want.

After the immediate family, all others form a line of vehicles following the hearse, according to the instructions given at the end of the Seonghwa ceremony.

At the site

At the cemetery, the pallbearers carry the casket from the hearse to the burial site, preceded by the person using Holy Salt and the picture bearer. Family and friends attending the burial may either proceed after the casket or gather at graveside. A pail or bucket of soil and small shovel should be prepared.

Service

The Wonjeon ceremony can be led by the same person who conducted the Seonghwa ceremony or another person can be chosen.

The general format is:

- Holy Song

- Representative prayer

- Sermon (or Hoondokhae reading)

- Words by significant leaders and/or members of immediate family

- Lowering of the casket

- Flower and soil offerings

- Closing prayer

- Cheers of Eog-Mansei: (1) For the beloved Heavenly Parent! (Hanul Pumo Nim) (2) For the victorious True Parents of

Heaven, Earth and Humankind! (Cham Pumo nim) (3) For the establishment of Cheon Il Guk! (4) (Optional) For (name of ascending individual)

Flower offering

Family and friends (everyone or representatives) place a flower on the casket.

Soil offering

Representatives of the immediate family offer a shovelful of soil on top of the casket. Other significant individuals may also do so. This recognizes that the body returns to the earth. The service ends with a closing prayer and three cheers of Eog mansei. The candles and incense are extinguished, if used.

Post-ceremony activities

The immediate family and all individuals participating in organizing and carrying out the ceremonies may want to dine together following the Wonjeon ceremony, or a reception may be organized at a convenient location. A funeral reception is sometimes called a "repast."

The immediate family takes home with them the individual's picture and candle used in the ceremony. There is no special ceremony when re-entering the home after any of the above ceremonies.

Checklists

Support Needed:

One or more community members who are friends of the family should be a central point between the Seonghwa Committee and the family. This helps ease the burden of many practical decisions.

Someone should:

- Help the family make arrangements for mortuary, casket, burial site, death certificates, etc.

- Coordinate prayer vigil and announcements to the community

- Help provide meals, transportation, etc. for family as needed

Someone should help the family:

- Write biography and/or obituary

- Gather photos for announcements and slideshow

- Prepare Powerpoint or presentation with favorite music

- Prepare a youcaring.com site for donations and Facebook page, if wanted.

- Design and print banner (for example, at www.staples.com) (2.5 x 4 ft for Fort Lincoln room.)

- Prepare information for program and design and print it.

- Choose who will serve as officiator for Seonghwa

- Choose who will serve as officiator for Wonjeon (may be same person)

- Choose who will:

    o Give testimonies at Seonghwa

    o Invocation at Seonghwa

    o Choose the songs

    o Deliver the Seonghwa address

    o Representative prayer at Wonjeon

    o Deliver a message or read Hoondokhae at Wonjeon

Day of service needs - Someone to Coordinate:

- Who will bring Seonghwa kit

- Who will set up altar – (at least 30 min before service)

- Who will serve as greeters and ushers – arrive early

- Who will take care of guest book and donation box (purchase or make)

- 6 people as pallbearers - after service at Fort Lincoln. If elsewhere, earlier for arrival of holy body.

- One close family member to serve as picture bearer – after service procession to Wonjeon.

- Who will serve as Holy Salter – (District or other Pastor) after service procession to Wonjeon.
- Purchase and gather materials

- Videotape and/or take pictures of ceremonies

- Coordinate a meal or reception after Wonjeon ceremony

Materials for family to gather and prepare:

- Individual's Holy Robe, white gloves, white socks, white undergarments (Holy Salt new items)

- Individual's Holy Handkerchief (place in casket at prayer time)

- Individual's Blessing Ring (optional)

- *Divine Principle* or Father's words (place in casket)

- Special items that the person liked (place in casket, optional)

- Framed picture of individual for service - 14 x 17" photo in matted frame for keepsake.

Seonghwa Committee Kit should contain:

- Two white oblong table cloths for altar

- Tripod or stand to hold picture

- Pink or white ribbon for picture

- One or two Cheon Il Guk candles, newly multiplied, and stands

- Family Federation or UC flag (place on top of casket during ceremony)

- Holy Salt in decorative dish/bowl

- White gloves (pallbearers, officiator, Holy Salter, & photo bearer)

- Incense and bowl with sand

- Matches or lighter

- Tape for flag

- Holy Song CD

Flowers and other items to prepare:

- Boutonnières - Red or pink for women. White for men. (Flowers for family and those in the program)

- Single assorted flowers for flower offering

- Flower arrangements (ordered by friends and family)

- Tape or pins to hang banner or sign

- Masking or scotch tape to secure flag on coffin

- Donation box

- Guest book

- Video camera and camera

- Sound system if needed

- Pail/bucket of soil and small shovel for soil offering

Approximate Costs

Prices will always increase, so the best way to save is by pre-planning. Begin to talk about it now!

In the case of Fort Lincoln Funeral Home and Fort Lincoln Cemetery, the location of our Wonjeon, their services are arranged through two offices: (1) The Funeral Home and (2) the Cemetery Office (building located nearest the entrance).[5]

- The Funeral Home: $6,500 for basic full service at the funeral home, and visitation (on day of service or prior day). The funeral home will pick up the deceased at the hospital, hospice, or home and prepare the body (bathe, dress) for viewing. This also includes a basic steel coffin, flowers, and miscellaneous expenses.

- The Cemetery Office: There are two major expenses. (1) $1,700 for the opening and closing of the crypt. This refers to the graveside ceremony with a canopy set up by the plot, chairs, and lowering of the casket after the service. (2) $2,300 for the bronze marker (16" x 24" on a granite base).

- Plus, the price of the crypt, which is purchased from HSA. Cost of the crypt ($2,500 for a two-person crypt or $2,000 for a single).

Summary: (all prices approximate based on 2014 costs)

Traditional burial using Fort Lincoln Funeral Home and Cemetery

$2,500	HSA-UWC – Two-person plot (or $2000 single). Payable to HSA-UWC in NY
6,500	Fort Lincoln Funeral Home - expenses, including the casket

---

[5] Other area cemeteries used by members: Parklawn Memorial Park and Gate of Heaven Cemetery in Montgomery County, MD.

4,000	Fort Lincoln Cemetery - services and marker
$13,000	**GRAND TOTAL FOR TRADITIONAL BURIAL** (If the two-person plot is already purchased, then the service for the surviving spouse would be less $2,500. The marker price would also be less.)

Cremation using Chambers Funeral Home for the cremation and burial of the ashes at Fort Lincoln.

$1,000	Cremation
445	Transfer of remains from Baltimore
200	Use of area for committal service (prayer before cremation)
275	Burial urn or use container provided by funeral home
58	Death certificates
$1,978	**TOTAL**

Cremation at Fort Lincoln Funeral Home and Cemetery (Brentwood, MD)

875	Cemetery burial
110	Administrative fee
60	Burial container installation (Tent, chairs, etc.)
2,500	HSA fee for four burial sites. Some families may purchase a plot for 4 cremations. Or $800 for a single cremation crypt.
1,579	Marker - Made of stone, not with brass plate like other markers (Fram Monument, Inc.)
600	Service was at New Hope Academy.

500	Food
$6,224	**TOTAL**
$8,202	**GRAND TOTAL FOR CREMATION**

If funeral and cemetery arrangements are made in advance (called pre-need or pre-planned), then you ensure that your final wishes are carried out, you spare your family the burden of making choices at a difficult time, and a payment plan can be arranged over time. If no prior arrangements are made and it's made at the time of death (called at-need), then full payment up front is required.

Markers

The marker may be purchased from Fort Lincoln or directly from the manufacturer (http://www.frammonument.com)

$2,395 - Option A: 24 x 14 - bronze on granite (installation, cemetery fee, unlimited text & emblems)

$1,495 - Option B: 28 x 18 - granite (grey, black, red, mahogany, pink)

$1495 - Option C
28 x 18 - granite

$795 – Option C: 24 x 12 - granite (grey)

Markers (may be purchased through Fort Lincoln or directly from the manufacturer, Fram Monument)

Fram Monument (Contact: Niv Fishbein @ niv@frammonument.com, (301) 605-8081 in Rockville, MD, Www.FramMonument.Com. Price includes installation, cemetery fee, unlimited text & emblems)

Post-Seonghwa Ceremony

Home Altar. The incense, candles, and picture used during the Seonghwa are set up on an altar at home. The immediate family offers prayers for at least the first 40 days.

Third Day Memorial Service

Sam Oje. The immediate family and any friends that wish to do so visit the Wonjeon to pray on the third day after the Wonjeon (day of the Wonjeon is day one). The spouse may lead the memorial service or ask someone else to do so. A food offering may be prepared in advance and placed on the grave.

Fortieth Day Memorial Service

Services may be offered at the burial site 21, 40, and 100 days after the ascension. In the Unification Church, holding a service on the 40th day has become the standard. When offering a memorial service at the burial site, prepare a small offering table and follow the order of the Seonghwa service. When offering a prayer, pray that the deceased person can lead a good life in the eternal Spirit World centered on God's will. Extenuating circumstances may not permit holding a service at the Wonjeon. Please know that the most important element of a Seonghwa is the attitude to release the loved one as he or she begins life in the Spirit World.

Annual return to the Wonjeon

According to Korean tradition, the spirit of the ascended individual returns to the Wonjeon on the anniversary of his or her death and sometimes on the birthday. The immediate family and any friends may return to the Wonjeon on those days to offer prayer, song, food, and share testimonies. If circumstances prevent visitations, then perform similar ceremonies at a home altar. There also should be an annual Chuseok (Korean Thanksgiving) celebration, which is organized by the local Seonghwa Committee.

Disposition of the donations received at the ceremonies.
These funds should be turned over to the family and used for expenses of the various ceremonies, including a donation to the church for incurred expenses.

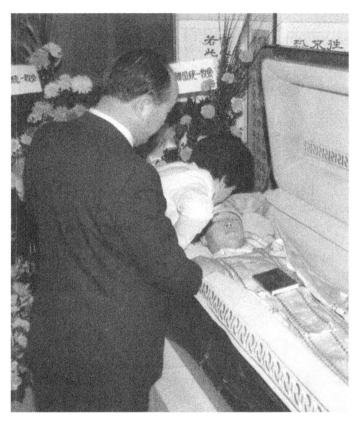

True Mother kisses Heung Jin Nim at ceremony in Belvedere on Jan. 2, 1984.

Guide to Preparation and Planning

The following section contains standardized forms to record personal information that is important for preparation and planning. Templates for a will, living will, and the Five Wishes are included as models.

Personal Information

Here is a summary of the key items you should have recorded and kept somewhere safe.

The list covers the basics, but add/edit/delete as you need based on your life. Confirm you have the items on hand, and jot down on the form below where they are located.

Remember: Let one or two people you trust know where this information can be accessed if necessary. Give a copy to the Power of Attorney listed in your will, and keep a copy of this with your other important documents (will, living will, policies and licenses, etc.)

These details belong to:

_____

They were last updated on:

_____

Your Basic info:

Full name:
_____

Address:
_____

Phone(s):
_____

Email(s):
_____

Birthday:
_____

Social Security #: _____

_____

Family Members contact info: Family, close friends, anyone listed in your Will and Living Will should be found here:

List: Full name, Relationship, Phone numbers, Email addresses, Home addresses, and any other relevant information

1. _____

2. _____

3. _____

Licenses and Policies: Confirm you have/need copies, and where located:

Bank names and
contact info: _____

Checking account(s): _____

Savings account(s): _____

Other bank account(s): _____

401k(s): _____

Other
savings/retirement
funds: _____

Stocks: _____

Accounts(s) on
autopay: _____

College savings (529
plan, etc.):

Debt (credit cards,
school loans):

Mortgage:

Marriage certificate:
(certified copy):

Birth certificate:

Car insurance:

Home insurance:

Life insurance:

Banking and Business:

Passwords:

Home computer username and passwords:

Laptop username and password:

Online banking accounts:

Cell phone password:

Email(s):

Social networking sites (Facebook, Flickr,
Linkedin, etc):

Online accounts (Netflix, iTunes, Amazon,
etc):

Medical and Health:

Medical Insurance: (company
and accounts):

_____

Medications:

_____

Existing Conditions:

_____

Allergies:

_____

Allergies to medications:

Primary Care Physician:

_____

Specialist(s):

_____

Therapist:

_____

Pediatrician:

_____

Other:

_____

My medical records are located:

_____

Other Information:

1. _____

2. _____

3. _____

Facts and Samples about Wills and Living Wills

http://www.nolo.com/legal-encyclopedia/sample-will.html

Will of Willa Willmaker

Part 1. Personal Information
I, Willa Willmaker, a resident of the State of California, Alameda County, declare that this is my will.

Part 2. Revocation of Previous Wills
I revoke all wills and codicils that I have previously made.

[This provision makes clear that this is the will to be used -- not any other wills or amendments to those wills, called codicils, that were made earlier. To prevent possible confusion, all earlier wills and codicils should also be physically destroyed.]

Part 3. Marital Status
I am married to Bob Willmaker.

[Here you identify your spouse if you are married -- or your partner, if you are in a registered domestic partnership, civil union or other marriage-like relationship recognized by your state.]

Part 5. Pets
I leave my Boston terrier, Clementine, and $1,500 to Jenny Amigo, with the hope that the money will be used for Clementine's care and maintenance. If Jenny Amigo does not survive me, I leave Clementine and $2,000 to Bob Smith, with the hope that the money will be used for Clementine's care and maintenance.

[Here you can leave your pet to a trusted caretaker. You can also leave money to the caretaker with a request that the caretaker use the money for your pet's care.]

Part 6. Disposition of Property
A beneficiary must survive me for at least 45 days to receive property under this will. As used in this will, the phrase "survive me" means to be alive or in existence as an organization on the 45th day after my death.

[This language means that to receive property under your will, a person must be alive for at least 45 days after your death.

Otherwise, the property will go to whomever you named as an alternate. This language permits you to choose another way to leave your property if your first choice dies within a short time after you do.

This will clause also prevents the confusion associated with the simultaneous death of spouses or domestic partners, when it is hard to tell who gets the property they have left to one another. Property left to a spouse or domestic partner who dies within 45 days of the other spouse or domestic partner, including a spouse or partner who dies simultaneously, will go to the person or organization named as alternate.]

If I leave property to be shared by two or more beneficiaries, and any of them does not survive me, I leave his or her share to the others equally unless this will provides otherwise.

[This clause states that if you leave a gift to two or more beneficiaries without stating the percentage each should receive, the beneficiaries will share the gift equally. This clause is included as a catchall; you can determine the shares for almost every shared gift.]

My residuary estate is all property I own at my death that is subject to this will that does not pass under a general or specific bequest, including all failed or lapsed requests.

[This definition is included so that you and your survivors are clear on the meaning of "residuary estate."]

I leave $10,000 to Gary Johnson. If Gary Johnson does not survive me, I leave this property to Suzie White.

[This language leaves a specific item of property -- $10,000 -- to a named beneficiary, Gary Johnson. If Gary Johnson does not survive the testator, then Suzie White will get the money.]

I leave my rare stamp collection to Jenny Amigo, Michael Swanson and Jose Gladstone as follows: Jenny Amigo shall receive a 1/4 share. Michael Swanson shall receive a 1/4 share. Jose Gladstone shall receive a 1/2 share.

[This language leaves a specific item of property -- a stamp collection -- to three people in unequal shares.]

I leave my collection of Nash cars to the Big Sky Auto Museum and Marcus Stone in equal shares. If Marcus Stone does not survive me, I leave his share of this property to Cyndy Stone.

[This will leaves specific property to an organization and a person equally. Since the testator here was concerned about providing for the possibility that the person would not survive to take the property, she named an alternate for him.]

I leave my residuary estate to my spouse, Bob Smith.

[This clause gives the residuary estate -- all property that does not pass under this will in specific bequests -- to the testator's spouse. Your residuary estate may be defined differently depending on your plans for leaving your property.]

If Bob Smith does not survive me, I leave my residuary estate to Ricky Willmaker and Gloria Willmaker in a children's pot trust to be administered under the children's pot trust provisions.

[If the person named here to take the residuary estate does not survive the testator, the residuary estate will pass to the two people named: the testator's children. The property will be put in one pot for the children to use as they mature. Specifics of how this pot trust operates are explained later in the will. Keep in mind that, in this example, the pot trust will come into being only if the testator's spouse does not survive the testator by at least 45 days.]

If both of these children are age 18 or older at my death, my residuary estate shall be distributed to them directly in equal shares.

[This clause makes clear what should happen if the children are older than the age at which the testator specified the pot trust should end. In this case, no pot trust will be created; the children will get the property directly and divide it evenly.]

If either of these children does not survive me, I leave his or her share to the other child.

[This clause explains that if either child does not survive, the other will get the property directly.]

If Bob Smith, Ricky Willmaker and Gloria Willmaker do not survive me, I leave my residuary estate to Christine Clemens.

All personal and real property that I leave in this will shall pass subject to any encumbrances or liens placed on the property as security for the repayment of a loan or debt.

[This language explains that whoever gets any property under this will also gets the mortgage and other legal claims against the property, such as liens. And anyone who takes property that is subject to a loan, such as a car loan, gets the debt as well as the property.]

Part 7. Forgiveness of Debts

I wish to forgive all debts specified below, plus accrued interest as of the date of my death: Sheila Jenkins, April 6, 2007, $10,000.

[Forgiving a debt is equivalent to making a bequest of money. It is a common way to equalize what you leave to all your children when you have loaned one of them some money -- that is, the amount that you would otherwise leave that child can be reduced by the amount of the debt being forgiven.]

Part 8. Executor

I name Bob Smith to serve as my executor. If Bob Smith is unwilling or unable to serve as executor, I name Jenny Amigo to serve as my executor.

No executor shall be required to post bond.

[This clause identifies the choices for executor and an alternate executor who will take over if the first choice is unable or unwilling to serve when the time comes.]

Part 9. Executor's Powers

I direct my executor to take all actions legally permissible to have the probate of my will done as simply and as free of court supervision as possible under the laws of the state having jurisdiction over this will, including filing a petition in the appropriate court for the independent administration of my estate.

[This clause sets out the specific authority that the executor will need to competently manage the estate until it has been distributed under the terms of the will. The will language expresses your desire that your executor work as free from court

supervision as possible. This will cut down on delays and expense.

When you print out your will, a second paragraph will list a number of specific powers that your executor will have, if necessary. It also makes clear that the listing of these specific powers does not deprive your executor of any other powers that he or she has under the law of your state. The general idea is to give your executor as much power as possible, so that he or she will not have to go to court and get permission to take a particular action.]

Part 10. Payment of Debts

Except for liens and encumbrances placed on property as security for the repayment of a loan or debt, I direct that all debts and expenses owed by my estate be paid using the following assets: Account #666777 at Cudahy Savings Bank.

[This clause states how debts will be paid. Depending on your choice when making your will, your debts may be paid either from specific assets you designate, or from your residuary estate -- all the property covered by your will that does not pass through a specific bequest.]

Part 11. Payment of Taxes

I direct that all estate and inheritance taxes assessed against property in my estate or against my beneficiaries to be paid using the following asset: Account #939494050 at the Independence Bank, Central Branch.

[This clause states how any estate or inheritance taxes owed by the estate or beneficiaries should be paid. You can choose whether your taxes should be paid from all of your property, from specific assets you designate or by your executor according to the law of your state.]

Part 12. No-Contest

If any beneficiary under this will contests this will or any of its provisions, any share or interest in my estate given to the contesting beneficiary under this will is revoked and shall be disposed of as if that contesting beneficiary had not survived me.

[This harsh-sounding clause is intended to discourage anyone who receives anything under the will from challenging its legality for the purpose of receiving a larger share. Many states will not

enforce a no-contest clause if the challenger has a good reason for the contest. Other states have passed laws specifically stating that a no-contest clause will not be enforced. If a court decides not to carry out the no-contest clause in your will, the rest of the document will be enforced as written.]

Part 13. Severability
If any provision of this will is held invalid, that shall not affect other provisions that can be given effect without the invalid provision.

[This is standard language that ensures that in the unlikely event that a court finds any individual part of your will to be invalid, the rest of the document will remain in effect.]

SIGNATURE
I, Willa Willmaker, the testator, sign my name to this instrument, this _____ day of _____, _____, at _____. I declare that I sign and execute this instrument as my last will, that I sign it willingly, and that I execute it as my free and voluntary act. I declare that I am of the age of majority or otherwise legally empowered to make a will, and under no constraint or undue influence.

Signature: _____

WITNESSES
We, the witnesses, sign our names to this document, and declare that the testator willingly signed and executed this document as the testator's last will.

In the presence of the testator, and in the presence of each other, we sign this will as witnesses to the testator's signing.

To the best of our knowledge, the testator is of the age of majority or otherwise legally empowered to make a will, is of sound mind and under no constraint or undue influence. We declare under penalty of perjury that the foregoing is true and correct, this _____ day of _____, _____, at _____.

First Witness
Sign your name:

_____

Print your name:

_____

Address:

_____

City, State:

_____

Second Witness

Sign your name:

_____

Print your name:

_____

Address:

_____

City, State:

_____

Sample of Living Will and the Five Wishes

Living Will

An advance health care directive, also known as a living will, personal directive, advance directive, or advance decision, is a legal document in which a person specifies what actions should be taken for their health if they are no longer able to make decisions for themselves because of illness or incapacity.

A living will is one form of advance directive, leaving instructions for treatment. Another form is a specific type of power of attorney or health care proxy, in which the person authorizes someone (an agent) to make decisions on their behalf when they are incapacitated. People are often encouraged to complete both documents to provide comprehensive guidance regarding their care. Examples of combination documents include the Five Wishes and MyDirectives advance directives in the United States.

- Review it: Read through it very carefully and make sure everything is clear to you. If you are confused, look it up or ask for help (or ask a lawyer).

- Sign it: In front of a notary, sign with two witnesses (not your spouse, relative, or anyone listed in this document).

The Five Wishes

The Five Wishes is a national (United States) advance directive created by the non-profit organization Aging with Dignity. It has been described as the "living will with a heart and soul."

MY WISH FOR:

- The Person I Want to Make Care Decisions for Me When I Can't
- The Kind of Medical Treatment I Want or Don't Want
- How Comfortable I Want to Be
- How I Want People to Treat Me
- What I Want My Loved Ones to Know

Name

Birthdate

There are many things in life that are out of our hands. This Five Wishes document gives you a way to control something very important: how you are treated if you get seriously ill. It is an easy-to-complete form that lets you say exactly what you want. Once it is filled out and properly signed it is valid under the laws of most states.

What Is Five Wishes?

Five Wishes is the first living will that talks about your personal, emotional, and spiritual needs as well as your medical wishes. It lets you choose the person you want to make health care decisions for you if you are not able to make them for yourself. Five Wishes lets you say exactly how you wish to be treated if you get seriously ill. It was written with the help of The American Bar Association's Commission on Law and Aging, and the nation's leading experts in end-of-life care. It's also easy to use. All you have to do is check a box, circle a direction, or write a few sentences.

How Five Wishes Can Help You and Your Family

- It lets you talk with your family, friends, and doctor about how you want to be treated if you become seriously ill.

- Your family members will not have to guess what you want. It protects them if you become seriously ill, because they won't have to make hard choices without knowing your wishes.

- You can know what your mom, dad, spouse, or friend wants. You can be there for them when they need you most. You will understand what they really want.

How Five Wishes Began

For 12 years, Jim Towey worked closely with Mother Teresa, and, for one year, he lived in a hospice she ran in Washington, DC. Inspired by this first-hand experience, Mr. Towey sought a way for patients and their families to plan ahead and to cope with serious illness. The result is Five Wishes and the response to it has been overwhelming. It has been featured on CNN and NBC's "Today" Show and in the pages of *Time* and *Money* magazines. Newspapers have called Five Wishes the first "living will with a heart and soul." Today, Five Wishes is available in 26 languages and in Braille.

Who Should Use Five Wishes

Five Wishes is for anyone 18 or older married, single, parents, adult children, and friends. More than 15 million people of all ages have already used it. Because it works so well, lawyers, doctors, hospitals and hospices, faith communities, employers, and retiree groups are handing out this document.

Five Wishes States

If you live in the District of Columbia or one of the 42 states listed below, you can use Five Wishes and have the peace of mind to know that it substantially meets your state's requirements under the law: Alaska, Arizona, Arkansas, California, Colorado, Connecticut, Delaware, Florida, Georgia, Hawaii, Idaho, Illinois, Iowa, Kentucky, Louisiana, Maine, Maryland, Massachusetts, Michigan, Minnesota, Mississippi, Missouri, Montana, Nebraska, Nevada, New Jersey, New Mexico, New York, North Carolina, North Dakota, Oklahoma, Pennsylvania, Rhode Island, South Carolina, South Dakota, Tennessee, Vermont, Virginia, Washington, West Virginia, Wisconsin, Wyoming.

If your state is not one of the 42 states listed here, Five Wishes does not meet the technical requirements in the statutes of your state. So some doctors in your state may be reluctant to honor Five Wishes. However, many people from states not on this list do complete Five Wishes along with their state's legal form. They find that Five Wishes helps them express all that they want and provides a helpful guide to family members, friends, caregivers, and doctors. Most doctors and health care professionals know they need to listen to your wishes no matter how you express them.

How Do I Change to Five Wishes?

You may already have a living will or a durable power of attorney for health care. If you want to use Five Wishes instead, all you need to do is fill out and sign a new Five Wishes as directed. As soon as you sign it, it takes away any advance directive you had before. To make sure the right form is used, please do the following:

- Destroy all copies of your old living will or durable power of attorney for health care. Or you can write "revoked" in large letters across the copy you have. Tell your lawyer if he or she helped prepare those old forms for you. AND

- Tell your Health Care Agent, family members, and doctor that you have filled out a new Five Wishes. Make sure they know about your new wishes.

WISH 1
The Person I Want To Make Health Care Decisions for Me When I Can't Make Them for Myself.

If I am no longer able to make my own health care decisions, this form names the person I choose to make these choices for me. This person will be my Health Care Agent (or other term that may be used in my state, such as proxy, representative, or surrogate). This person will make my health care choices if both of these things happen:

- My attending or treating doctor finds I am no longer able to make health care choices, AND

- Another health care professional agrees that this is true.

If my state has a different way of finding that I am not able to make health care choices, then my state's way should be followed.

The Person I Choose As My Health Care Agent Is:

_____   _____
First Choice Name   phone

_____   _____
Address   City/State/Zip

If this person is not able or willing to make these choices for me, OR is divorced or legally separated from me, OR this person has died, then these people are my next choices:

_____   _____
Second Choice Name   phone

_____   _____
Address   City/State/Zip

_____   _____
Third Choice Name   phone

_____   _____
Address   City/State/Zip

Picking the Right Person to Be Your Health Care Agent

Choose someone who knows you very well, cares about you, and who can make difficult decisions. A spouse or family member may not be the best choice because they are too emotionally involved. Sometimes they are the best choice. You know best. Choose someone who is able to stand up for you so that your wishes are followed. Also, choose someone who is likely to be nearby so that they can help when you need them. Whether you choose a spouse, family member, or friend as your Health Care Agent, make sure you talk about these wishes and be sure that this person agrees to respect and follow your wishes. Your Health Care Agent should be at least 18 years or older (in Colorado, 21 years or older) and should not be:

- Your health care provider, including the owner or operator of a health or residential or community care facility serving you.

- An employee or spouse of an employee of your health care provider.

- Serving as an agent or proxy for 10 or more people unless he or she is your spouse or close relative.

I understand that my Health Care Agent can make health care decisions for me. I want my Agent to be able to do the following: (please cross out anything you don't want your Agent to do that is listed below.)

- Make choices for me about my medical care or services, like tests, medicine, or surgery. This care or service could be to find out what my health problem is, or how to treat it. It can also include care to keep me alive. If the treatment or care has already started, my Health Care Agent can keep it going or have it stopped.

- Interpret any instructions I have given in this form or given in other discussions, according to my Health Care Agent's understanding of my wishes and values.

- Consent to admission to an assisted living facility, hospital, hospice, or nursing home for me. My Health Care Agent can

60

hire any kind of health care worker I may need to help me or take care of me. My Agent may also fire a health care worker, if needed.

- Make the decision to request, take away, or not give medical treatments, including artificially provided food and water, and any other treatments to keep me alive.

- See and approve release of my medical records and personal files. If I need to sign my name to get any of these files, my Health Care Agent can sign it for me.

- Move me to another state to get the care I need or to carry out my wishes.

- Authorize or refuse to authorize any medication or procedure needed to help with pain.

- Take any legal action needed to carry out my wishes.

- Donate useable organs or tissues of mine as allowed by law.

- Apply for Medicare, Medicaid, or other programs or insurance benefits for me. My Health Care Agent can see my personal files, like bank records, to find out what is needed to fill out these forms.

- Listed below are any changes, additions, or limitations on my Health Care Agent's powers.

_____

_____

If I Change My Mind about Having A Health Care Agent, I Will

- Destroy all copies of this part of the Five Wishes form. OR

- Tell someone, such as my doctor or family, that I want to cancel or change my Health Care Agent. OR

- Write the word "Revoked" in large letters across the name of each agent whose authority I want to cancel. Sign my name on that page.

WISH 2
My Wish For The Kind Of Medical Treatment I Want Or Don't Want.

I believe that my life is precious and I deserve to be treated with dignity. When the time comes that I am very sick and am not able to speak for myself, I want the following wishes, and any other directions I have given to my Health Care Agent, to be respected and followed.

What You Should Keep In Mind as My Caregiver

- I do not want to be in pain. I want my doctor to give me enough medicine to relieve my pain, even if that means that I will be drowsy or sleep more than I would otherwise.

- I do not want anything done or omitted by my doctors or nurses with the intention of taking my life.

- I want to be offered food and fluids by mouth, and kept clean and warm.

What "Life-Support Treatment" Means to Me

Life-support treatment means any medical procedure, device or medication to keep me alive. Life-support treatment includes: medical devices put in me to help me breathe; food and water supplied by medical device (tube feeding); cardiopulmonary resuscitation (CPR); major surgery; blood transfusions; dialysis; antibiotics; and anything else meant to keep me alive. If I wish to limit the meaning of life-support treatment because of my religious or personal beliefs, I write this limitation in the space below. I do this to make very clear what I want and under what conditions.

_____

_____

In Case of an Emergency

If you have a medical emergency and ambulance personnel arrive, they may look to see if you have a Do Not Resuscitate form or bracelet. Many states require a person to have a Do Not Resuscitate form filled out and signed by a doctor. This form lets ambulance personnel know that you don't want them to use life-support treatment when you are dying. Please check with your doctor to see if you need to have a Do Not Resuscitate form filled out.

Here is the kind of medical treatment that I want or don't want in the four situations listed below. I want my Health Care Agent, my family, my doctors and other health care providers, my friends and all others to know these directions.

Close to death:

If my doctor and another health care professional both decide that I am likely to die within a short period of time, and life-support treatment would only delay the moment of my death (Choose one of the following):

- I want to have life-support treatment.

- I do not want life-support treatment. If it has been started, I want it stopped.

- I want to have life-support treatment if my doctor believes it could help. But I want my doctor to stop giving me life-support treatment if it is not helping my health condition or symptoms.

In a Coma and Not Expected to Wake Up or Recover:

If my doctor and another health care professional both decide that I am in a coma from which I am not expected to wake up or recover, and I have brain damage, and life-support treatment would only delay the moment of my death (Choose one of the following):

- I want to have life-support treatment.

- I do not want life-support treatment. If it has been started, I want it stopped.

- I want to have life-support treatment if my doctor believes it could help. But I want my doctor to stop giving me life-support treatment if it is not helping my health condition or symptoms.

Permanent and Severe Brain Damage and Not Expected to Recover:

If my doctor and another health care professional both decide that I have permanent and severe brain damage, (for example, I can open my eyes, but I cannot speak or understand) and I am not expected to get better, and life-support treatment would only delay the moment of my death (Choose one of the following):

- I want to have life-support treatment.

- I do not want life-support treatment. If it has been started, I want it stopped.

- I want to have life-support treatment if my doctor believes it could help. But I want my doctor to stop giving me life-support treatment if it is not helping my health condition or symptoms.

In Another Condition Under Which I Do Not Wish t Be Kept Alive:

If there is another condition under which I do not wish to have life-support treatment, I describe it below. In this condition, I believe that the costs and burdens of life-support treatment are too much and not worth the benefits to me. Therefore, in this condition, I do not want life-support treatment. (For example, you may write "end-stage condition." That means that your health has gotten worse. You are not able to take care of yourself in any way, mentally or physically. Life-support treatment will not help you recover. Please leave the space blank if you have no other condition to describe.)

_____

_____

The next three wishes deal with my personal, spiritual, and emotional wishes. They are important to me. I want to be treated with dignity near the end of my life, so I would like people to do the things written in Wishes 3, 4, and 5 when they can be done. I understand that my family, my doctors and other health care providers, my friends, and others may not be able to do these things or are not required by law to do these things. I do not expect the following wishes to place new or added legal duties on my doctors or other health care providers. I also do not expect these wishes to excuse my doctor or other health care providers from giving me the proper care asked for by law.

WISH 3
My Wish for How Comfortable I Want to Be.
(Please cross out anything that you don't agree with.)

- I do not want to be in pain. I want my doctor to give me enough medicine to relieve my pain, even if that means I will be drowsy or sleep more than I would otherwise.

- If I show signs of depression, nausea, shortness of breath, or hallucinations, I want my caregivers to do whatever they can to help me.

- I wish to have a cool moist cloth put on my head if I have a fever.

- I want my lips and mouth kept moist to stop dryness.

- I wish to have warm baths often. I wish to be kept fresh and clean at all times.

- I wish to be massaged with warm oils as often as I can be to avoid itching.

- I wish to have my favorite music played when possible, until my time of death.

- I wish to have personal care like shaving, nail clipping, hair brushing, and teeth brushing, as long as they do not cause me pain or discomfort.

- I wish to have religious readings and well-loved poems read aloud when I am near death.

- I want my lips and mouth kept moist.

- I wish to know about options for hospice care to provide medical, emotional, and spiritual care for me and my loved ones.

WISH 4
My Wish for How I Want People to Treat Me.
(Cross out anything that you don't agree with.)

- I wish to have people with me when possible. I want someone to be with me when it seems that death may come at any time.

- I wish to have my hand held and to be talked to when possible, even if I don't seem to respond to the voice or touch of others.

- I wish to have others by my side praying for me when possible.

- I wish to have the members of my faith community told that I am sick and asked to pray for me and visit me.

- I wish to be cared for with kindness and cheerfulness, and not sadness.

- I wish to have pictures of my loved ones in my room, near my bed.

- If I am not able to control my bowel or bladder functions, I wish for my clothes and bed linens to be kept clean, and for them to be changed as soon as they can be if they have been soiled.

- I want to die in my home, if that can be done.

WISH 5
My Wish for What I Want My Loved Ones to Know.
(Cross out anything that you don't agree with.)

- I wish to have my family and friends know that I love them.

- I wish to be forgiven for the times I have hurt my family, friends, and others.

- I wish to have my family, friends, and others know that I forgive them for when they may have hurt me in my life.

- I wish for my family and friends to know that I do not fear death itself. I think it is not the end, but a new beginning for me.

- I wish for all of my family members to make peace with each other before my death, if they can.

- I wish for my family and friends to think about what I was like before I became seriously ill. I want them to remember me in this way after my death.

- I wish for my family and friends and caregivers to respect my wishes even if they don't agree with them.

- I wish for my family and friends to look at my dying as a time of personal growth for everyone, including me. This will help me live a meaningful life in my final days.

- I wish for my family and friends to get counseling if they have trouble with my death. I want memories of my life to give them joy and not sorrow.

- After my death, I would like my body to be (mark or circle one): buried or cremated.

- My body or remains should be put in the following location: Fort Lincoln Funeral Home and Cemetery, 3401 Bladensburg Road, Brentwood, MD 20722.

- The following person knows my funeral wishes:

_____

_____

If anyone asks how I want to be remembered, please say the following about me:

_____

_____

If there is to be a memorial service for me, I wish for this service to include the following (list music, songs, readings or other specific requests that you have):

_____

_____

(Use the space below for any other wishes. For example, you may want to donate any or all parts of your body when you die. You may also wish to designate a charity to receive memorial contributions. Please attach a separate sheet of paper if you need more space.)

_____

_____

Signing the Five Wishes Form

Please make sure you sign your Five Wishes form in the presence of the two witnesses.

I, (name), ask that my family, my doctors, and other health care providers, my friends, and all others, follow my wishes as communicated by my Health Care Agent (if I have one and he or she is available), or as otherwise expressed in this form. This form becomes valid when I am unable to make decisions or speak for myself. If any part of this form cannot be legally followed, I ask that all other parts of this form be followed. I also revoke any health care advance directives I have made before.

Signature: _____Social Security: _____
Address:_____
Phone: _____Date: _____

Witness Statement - (2 witnesses needed):

I, the witness, declare that the person who signed or acknowledged this form (hereafter "person") is personally known to me, that he/she signed or acknowledged this [Health Care Agent and/or Living Will form(s)] in my presence, and that he/she appears to be of sound mind and under no duress, fraud, or undue influence.

I also declare that I am over 18 years of age and am NOT:

- The individual appointed as (agent/proxy/ surrogate/patient advocate/representative) by this document or his/her successor,

- The person's health care provider, including owner or operator of a health, long-term care, or other residential or community care facility serving the person,

- An employee of the person's health care provider,

- Financially responsible for the person's health care,

- An employee of a life or health insurance provider for the person,

- Related to the person by blood, marriage, or adoption, and,

- To the best of my knowledge, a creditor of the person or entitled to any part of his/her estate under a will or codicil, by operation of law.

(Some states may have fewer rules about who may be a witness. Unless you know your state's rules, please follow the above.)

_____   _____
Signature of Witness #1   Signature of Witness #2

_____   _____
Printed Name of Witness   Printed Name of Witness

_____   _____
Address   Address

_____   _____
Phone   Phone

Notarization - Only required for residents of Missouri, North Carolina, South Carolina and West Virginia

- If you live in Missouri, only your signature should be notarized.

- If you live in North Carolina, South Carolina or West Virginia, you should have your signature, and the signatures of your witnesses, notarized.

STATE OF _____ COUNTY OF _____. On this _____ day of _____, 20__, the said _____, and _____, known to me (or satisfactorily proven) to be the person named in the foregoing instrument and witnesses, respectively, personally appeared before me, a Notary Public, within and for the State and County aforesaid, and acknowledged that they freely and voluntarily executed the same for the purposes stated therein.

My Commission Expires:

_____
Notary Public

What to Do After You Complete Five Wishes

- Make sure you sign and witness the form just the way it says in the directions. Then your Five Wishes will be legal and valid.

- Talk about your wishes with your health care agent, family members, and others who care about you. Give them copies of your completed Five Wishes.

- Keep the original copy you signed in a special place in your home. Do NOT put it in a safe deposit box. Keep it nearby so that someone can find it when you need it.

- Fill out the wallet card below. Carry it with you. That way people will know where you keep your Five Wishes.

- Talk to your doctor during your next office visit. Give your doctor a copy of your Five Wishes. Make sure it is put in your medical record. Be sure your doctor understands your wishes and is willing to follow them. Ask him or her to tell other doctors who treat you to honor them.

- If you are admitted to a hospital or nursing home, take a copy of your Five Wishes with you. Ask that it be put in your medical record.

- I have given the following people copies of my completed Five Wishes:

_____

_____

If you live in certain institutions (a nursing home, other licensed long- term care facility, a home for the mentally retarded or developmentally disabled, or a mental health institution) in one of the states listed above, you may have to follow special "witnessing requirements" for your Five Wishes to be valid. For further information, please contact a social worker or patient advocate at your institution.

Five Wishes is meant to help you plan for the future. It is not meant to give you legal advice. It does not try to answer all questions about anything that could come up. Every person is different, and every situation is different. Laws change from time to time. If you have a specific question or problem, talk to a medical or legal professional for advice.

My primary care physician is:

_____
Name

_____
Address   City/State/Zip Phone   Email

My document is located:_____

Unification Church Burial Rights Agreement

This Agreement is made between HSA-UWC and

Name: _____

Address: _____

E-mail: _____ Phone: _____

The Seller agrees to sell and the Purchaser(s) agrees to buy, subject to the terms and conditions set out below, the following burial rights for the burial of human remains only and not for speculation, described as lawn crypt burial rights with accompanying rights and obligations as may be agreed upon between Seller and Fort Lincoln Cemetery.
Purchaser(s) agrees to pay (check one).

☐ $2000 - Single Crypt Site   ☐ $2500 - Double Crypt Site

For a plot in the Unification Church section (between the Historic Garden Mausoleum and the Garden of Grace) at Fort Lincoln Cemetery, 3401 Bladensburg Road, Brentwood, MD 20722

Payment Options: Check _____ Credit Card_____ (use CC authorization form)

Whereas this cemetery section is reserved for burial of members of the Unification Church, it is agreed that no purchase or transfer will be effective without prior written authorization by the Unification Church.

In the event that Purchaser(s) desires to relinquish the above rights and seek reimbursement of monies paid, such may be done at the discretion of the local Unification Church who will assume responsibility for reimbursement and/or resale. If granted, monies reimbursed will not exceed monies paid. The obligations of this Agreement shall take precedence over any provision in any other agreement between the parties in conflict with this Agreement.

_____   _____

(Purchaser's Signature)   (Administrator's Signature)

_____   _____
Printed Name   Printed Name

Date: _____   Date: _____

Contacts: Rev. Randy Francis (rfrancis@unification.org), Rev. Greg Carter (gcarter@unification.org), Dr. William Selig (wmselig@gmail.com) in Washington, DC, and treasurer, Mrs. Shizuko Iwaya (siwaya@unification.org) at HSA-UWC National Headquarters, 4 West 43rd St. New York, NY 10036.

Credit Card and Authorization Form

National Wonjeon Shrine
HSA-UWC of America

I, _____ hereby authorize HSA-UWC
to charge to the indicated credit card for donation purposes.

Purpose of Donation or Payment: _____

Card Type: Visa_____MasterCard_____ Amex _____

Card
Number:_____

Expiration Date of Card: _____ Sec Code: _____

Billing Address (Street): _____

City: _____   State:_____ Zip:_____

Phone Number:_____

Amount Authorized:_____ Please include a 3%
bank processing fee.

I, the undersigned, am the authorized cardholder for the credit
card indicated above, and my signature below authorizes the
charges to be billed to my credit card for the current billing cycle.

_____   _____
             Signature   Date

Please retain a copy for your records.

Contacts: Rev. Randy Francis (rfrancis@unification.org), Rev.
Greg Carter (gcarter@unification.org), Dr. William Selig
(wmselig@gmail.com) in Washington, DC, and treasurer, Mrs.
Shizuko Iwaya (siwaya@unification.org) at HSA-UWC National
Headquarters, 4 West 43rd St. New York, NY 10036.

Glossary

Aju - a term created by Father Moon. The word is used after a prayer like Amen, but with an important providential meaning related to ownership. Father translated it as: "I am the owner of this universe.... I can live as a true human being."

Ascension – refers to the spirit person's transition from earth to heaven.

At-need funeral arrangements – taking care of the funeral arrangements at the time of death.

Blessing/Marriage Blessing - The ceremony of rebirth that signifies reconnecting with the original untainted lineage that the Messiah couple brings.

Cheers of Eog-Mansei – Congratulatory cheers for ten thousand years of peace and happiness.

Cheon Il Guk - A Unification term for the Nation of Cosmic Peace and Unity or the Kingdom of God on earth.

Cheongpyeong Heaven and Earth Training Center – The Family Federation for World Peace and Unification spiritual retreat and holy ground in Korea.

Divine Principle – Main theological textbook of the Unification Church.

Dr. Sang Hun Lee – (1914-1997), a Unificationist, who after transitioning to the spirit world witnessed to many historic figures about the True Parents.

Heung Jin Moon - (Oct. 23, 1966 – Jan. 2, 1984), second son of the founders, died at age 17 in an auto accident.

Holy handkerchief – The Holy handkerchief, which has been sprinkled with holy wine (symbolizing parents' love), is given to members who have gone through both the engagement and holy wine ceremony.

Holy Salt - a sacrament of the Unification Church. By using blessed salt, we take things from Satan's world and ask God to accept them under His dominion. Prayer for the purification of items and places with the Cheon Il Guk Holy Salt. "I sanctify (name of item or place) in the name of our Heavenly Parent, the Parents of Heaven and Earth, and (your name), owner of Cheon Il Guk, Aju."

Hoon Dok Hae - a Korean expression meaning "Gathering for Reading and Learning," refers to the regular study of the spiritual guidance given by Father and Mother.

Marker – a marker placed on a grave to identify the person buried there.

National Wonjeon Shrine of America – Cemetery located in Brentwood, MD sanctified on May 14, 2002, blessed on July 26, 2002, and dedicated on October 9, 2003 as the final resting place for Blessed members.

Original homeland - The world as God originally envisioned.

Pre-need (pre-planned or pre-paid) arrangements – means taking care of the funeral and/or burial in advance.

Repast – a gathering of family and friends for a meal after a burial service.

Seonghwa – A term created by Father consisting of the Chinese characters seong meaning "holy" and hwa meaning "harmony."

Shimjung – a Korean term which translates as Heart.

Spirit World – A separate world that interfaces with the Physical World.

The Family Federation for World Peace and Unification (FFWPU) is the official name for the religious movement popularly known as the Unification Church.

The 3 Stages of Life – defined by True Father as the 9 months in the womb, the 90 years in the physical world, and the eternal life in the spirit world.

True love - Love that is given unconditionally; God's perfect love.

True Parent(s) - The first person/couple to actualize God's ideal of true love, that is, to reach complete spiritual maturity, as it is the potential of each of us to do.

Unification Church - The Unification Church (Holy Spirit Association for the Unification of World Christianity) was formally established in Seoul, Korea, on May 1, 1954. The first missionaries to the United States included: Young Oon Kim (1914-1989), David S.C. Kim (1915-2011), and Bo Hi Pak (1930-). HSA-UWC was legally founded on September 18,

1961, in California by Dr. Young Oon Kim, the first missionary. Dr. David S.C. Kim, the second missionary, founded the "United Faith, Inc." in Portland, Oregon, in 1961, and Col. Bo Hi Pak, the third missionary, incorporated the HSA-UWC in Arlington, Virginia, in 1963.

Father's Words
"Understanding Life and Death"
Washington, DC - December 18, 1998

Someday I, too, will die. When we are young, we don't think much about death. But we become increasingly serious about death as we grow older. This is because death is a gate through which we are inevitably destined to pass. But what happens to us after we die? Do you know why I am talking about death? I talk about death in order to teach the meaning of life. Who really knows the value of life? It is not the person who is going all out to preserve his life. The only person who really knows about life is the one who goes into the valley of death. He confirms the meaning of life as he desperately cries out to Heaven at the crossroads of life and death.

Why do people fear death? It is because they do not know the purpose for which we are born. Those who do not know why we are born do not know why we die. Therefore the first questions philosophers ask are "What is life? Why are we born?" If we think about it, we realize that when we die we are reborn into the midst of God's love. But in the human world, people cry out, "Oh no, I'm going to die! What am I to do?" They make a big fuss. Do you think that God laughs, "Ho ho ho!" when we die? Or do you think God cries out, "Oh no!" and is overwhelmed with sorrow? The truth is, He is happy. This is because the moment of the physical body's death is the moment we experience the joy of leaving the finite realm of love in order enter the infinite realm of love. It is the moment of our second birth.

Then is God happier on the day we are born into the physical world, or at that moment we leave our physical body behind? At that moment, we are born a second time into the realm of the infinite expansion of love. We become His new children through death. Of course, God is happier at the second birth. I am telling you this because you need to know that you cannot have a relationship with God unless you are released from the fear of death.

Notes

Made in the USA
Las Vegas, NV
11 September 2022

55072459R00049